THE PRACTICAL STRATEGIES SERIES
IN GIFTED EDUCATION

series editors
FRANCES A. KARNES & KRISTEN R. STEPHENS

Identifying Gifted Students

A Step-by-Step Guide

Susan K. Johnsen

Routledge
Taylor & Francis Group

NEW YORK AND LONDON

First published 2005 by Prufrock Press Inc.

Published 2021 by Routledge
605 Third Avenue, New York, NY 10017
2 Park Square, Milton Park, Abingdon, Oxon OX14 4RN

Routledge is an imprint of the Taylor & Francis Group, an informa business

ISBN 13: 978-1-59363-174-1 (pbk)

Contents

The *Practical Strategies Series in Gifted Education* offers teachers, counselors, administrators, parents, and other interested parties up-to-date instructional techniques and information on a variety of issues pertinent to the field of gifted education. Each guide addresses a focused topic and is written by scholars with authority on the issue. Several guides have been published. Among the titles are:

- *Acceleration Strategies for Teaching Gifted Learners*
- *Curriculum Compacting: An Easy Start to Differentiating for High-Potential Students*
- *Enrichment Opportunities for Gifted Learners*
- *Independent Study for Gifted Learners*
- *Motivating Gifted Students*
- *Questioning Strategies for Teaching the Gifted*
- *Social & Emotional Teaching Strategies*
- *Using Media & Technology With Gifted Learners*

For a current listing of available guides within the series, please contact Prufrock Press at (800) 998-2208 or visit http://www.prufrock.com.

This publication will provide directors and coordinators of programs for gifted and talented students with a specific step-by-step plan for developing an identification procedure in a school or school district. While the sections of this publication are laid out sequentially according to the steps, identification is an ongoing process. For example, more complexity and depth in the curriculum may create opportunities for new students to be identified. New program options in the visual and performing arts may uncover the talents of budding artists. Some students may transfer into the school, while others may furlough or exit from the gifted program. In all cases, the goal of identification is to ensure that every gifted and talented student who needs a program that is different from the general education curriculum receives one that is matched to his or her specific characteristics.

Before beginning the step-by-step plan, administrators will want to form a committee that will collaborate in designing the identification procedure. This committee should be comprised of the coordinator or director of the gifted program, principals who are respected among their colleagues, teachers in gifted and in general education, parents who are active in the school community, and any other administrators who need to be involved to ensure the success of the plan.

This guide is organized around the following sequence of steps that a committee might follow in establishing an identification procedure:

Step 1:   Identify characteristics of gifted and talented students and program options.

Step 2:   Select multiple assessments that match these characteristics and programs.

Step 3:   Develop an identification procedure that ensures equal access.

Step 4:   Implement the identification procedure.

Step 5:   Organize assessment information, interpret results, and select students.

Step 6:   Evaluate and revise assessment procedures.

This publication is organized into six sections:

Identifying Characteristics of Gifted and Talented Students and Program Options—emphasizes the heterogeneity of this special group. Specific characteristics are provided for each of the areas in the federal definition of giftedness: general intellectual ability, specific academic fields, leadership, creativity, and the arts. Possible program options are then matched to these characteristics.

Selecting Multiple Assessments—begins with a discussion of the need for multiple assessments. Specific criteria are then presented to assist the identification committee in determining the technical adequacy of quantitative and qualitative assessments.

Developing an Identification Procedure That Ensures Equal Access—describes the three phases of identification (nomination, screening, and selection), followed by a brief overview of due process procedures. A specific checklist developed by the Office for Civil Rights is included so that districts may ensure equal access at each phase of the identification procedure.

Implementing the Identification Procedure—outlines an implementation calendar. Involvement of important stakeholders and the board of trustees is also emphasized along with professional development of everyone involved in the identification process.

Organizing Assessment Information, Interpreting Results, and Selecting Students—provides a variety of forms used in organizing assessment information. Example cases illustrate three different formats: case study, minimum scores, and profiles. Each of these formats also incorporates important guidelines for ensuring technical adequacy.

Evaluating and Revising Assessment Procedures—examines the important activity of evaluation. Six steps are outlined: (1) identifying evaluation questions, (2) selecting data sources and instruments, (3) matching the methods with the evaluation questions, (4) interpreting data, (5) writing the report, and (6) implementing recommendations.

I would like to thank directors of gifted and talented programs who have shared their successes (and a few failures) in developing effective identification procedures for their school districts. This publication will be useful in finding those students who require a gifted education.

Identifying Characteristics of Gifted
and Talented Students and Program Options

The first step in establishing a comprehensive program for gifted and talented students is for the identification committee to become familiar with the characteristics of gifted and talented students and specific program options that might match these characteristics. For example, consider the following students:

- James is a kindergarten student who is already reading at the fifth-grade level and solving math problems at the fourth-grade level. His teacher says that he is particularly interested in black holes and frequents the science section of the school library. While small for his age, he is also interested in athletics, having memorized all of the player statistics of the local football teams.

- LaTasha began taking music lessons at age 4. By the time she was 8, she was a proficient cellist, playing in the statewide youth symphony, which was quite an honor since all of the other performers were high school students. LaTasha has already decided that she wants to be a professional musician.

- Brandon was retained in two grades at the primary level because he didn't pass the grade-level reading assessments. His fourth-grade teacher was concerned because he wasn't making progress, and she didn't want him to fail again. The assistant principal in the school had observed Brandon and felt that he was choosing not to perform in the regular classroom. She decided to administer a reading test to Brandon in her office and discovered that he was actually reading on the sixth-grade level. She also found that he performed in the top 1% on a creativity test. After a parent conference, the school learned that Brandon had been putting his time and energy into building a rocket at home using scraps from garbage cans.

- Amanda was part of a team of students whose teacher required them to research the needs of their community. Upon finding that no affordable retirement homes were available to the elderly, she decided to organize a fund-raising campaign to change the situation. By the time she was finished, one of the community leaders had donated land for the project, while others had matched initial contributions. Within 2 years, the retirement home was built and ready for occupants.

All of these vignettes are based on true stories of gifted students and show the variety of characteristics they might exhibit. This variation is apparent in the United States federal definition of gifted and talented students:

The term "gifted and talented" when used in respect to students, children, or youth means students, children, or youth who give evidence of high performance capability in areas such as intellectual, creative, artistic, or leadership capacity, or in specific academic fields, and who require services or activities not ordinarily provided by the school in order to fully develop such capabilities. (P.L. 103-382, Title XIV, p. 388)

In the described cases, James gives evidence of high performance capability in intellectual and specific academic fields; Brandon in creativity; LaTasha in the arts; and Amanda in leadership. While each of the students provides examples that would indicate a gift or talent, not all perform equally well in the school setting. In fact, Brandon might have been overlooked except for the astute observations of an assistant principal. Those who are involved in the identification of students will want to consider the environment as an important influencing factor on student behaviors.

The majority of professionals in gifted education would agree that abilities are not exhibited independently of the environment or other factors. Tannenbaum (1983) identified these influencing factors as general ability (e.g., general intelligence), special ability (e.g., aptitude in a specific area), nonintellective facilitators (e.g., mental learning, commitment, strong self-concept, mental health, willingness to sacrifice), environmental influences (e.g., parents, classroom, peers, culture, social class), and chance. Similarly, Gagné (1995, 1999) has described the development of gifts into talents as being facilitated by intrapersonal and environmental catalysts. Intrapersonal catalysts are influenced by genetic background and include physical (e.g., health, physical appearance) and psychological (e.g., motivation, personality, and volition) factors. Environmental catalysts are surroundings (e.g., geographic, demographic, sociological), people (e.g., parents, teachers, siblings, peers), undertakings (e.g., programs for gifted and talented students), and events (e.g., divorce, changing schools, winning an award). In identifying gifted and talented students, observers need to consider not only the characteristic lists that are presented in this section, but also the opportunities that a student might have in exhibiting these characteristics.

Characteristics of Gifted Students

The characteristics of gifted and talented students are organized around the federal definition. These lists are summaries of characteristics noted by researchers in the field of gifted education.

General Intellectual Ability

Students who have general intellectual ability tend to show the potential to perform well in more than one area. Researchers have identified the following characteristics as relating to this area of giftedness:

- has an extensive and detailed memory, particularly in an area of interest;
- has vocabulary advanced for age—precocious language;
- has communication skills advanced for age and is able to express ideas and feelings;
- asks intelligent questions;
- is able to identify the important characteristics of new concepts and problems;
- learns information quickly;
- uses logic in arriving at common sense answers;
- has a broad base of knowledge—a large quantity of information;
- understands abstract ideas and complex concepts;
- uses analogical thinking, problem solving, or reasoning;
- observes relationships and sees connections;
- finds and solves difficult and unusual problems;
- understands principles, forms generalizations, and uses them in new situations;
- wants to learn and is curious;

- works conscientiously and has a high degree of concentration in areas of interest;
- understands and uses various symbol systems; and
- is reflective about learning (Clark, 1997; Colangelo & Davis, 1991; Coleman & Cross, 2001; Davis & Rimm, 1994; Gilliam, Carpenter, & Christensen, 1996; Khatena, 1992; Piirto, 1999; Renzulli, Smith, White, Callahan, Harman, & Westberg, 2002; Rogers, 2001; Ryser & McConnell, 2004; Sternberg & Davidson, 1986; Swassing, 1985; Tannenbaum, 1983).

Specific Academic Field

Some gifted and talented students exhibit potential or demonstrated accomplishment in one specific field of study. Such a student tends to exhibit these characteristics:

General (demonstrated within field of interest)
- has an intense, sustained interest;
- has hobbies/collections related to field;
- is attracted to cognitive complexity—enjoys solving complex problems;
- prefers classes/careers in the academic field;
- is highly self-motivated and persistent;
- has a broad base of knowledge;
- reads widely in an academic field;
- learns information quickly;
- has an inquisitive nature and asks good questions;
- examines and recalls details;
- recognizes critical elements and details in learning concepts;
- analyzes problems and considers alternatives;
- understands abstract ideas and concepts;
- uses vocabulary beyond grade level;
- verbalizes complex concepts and processes;

- visualizes images and translates into other forms—written, spoken, symbolic—music notation, numbers, letters; and
- sees connections and relationships in a field and generalizes to other situations and applications (Feldhusen, Hoover, & Sayler, 1989; Gilliam et al., 1996; Piirto, 1999; Ryser & McConnell, 2004; Rogers, 2001; Tannenbaum, 1983).

Math/Science
- is interested in numerical analysis;
- has a good memory for storing main features of problems and solutions;
- appreciates parsimony, simplicity, or economy in solutions;
- reasons effectively and efficiently;
- solves problems intuitively using insight;
- can reverse steps in the mental process;
- organizes data and experiments to discover patterns or relationships;
- improvises with science equipment and math methods; and
- is flexible in solving problems.

Social Studies/Language Arts
- enjoys language/verbal communication—communication skills;
- engages in intellectual play, enjoys puns, has a good sense of humor;
- organizes ideas and sequences in preparation for speaking and writing;
- suspends judgment, entertains alternative points of view;
- is original and creative—has unique ideas in writing or speaking;
- is sensitive to social, ethical, and moral issues;
- is interested in theories of causation;

- likes independent study and research in areas of interest; and
- uses these qualities in writing—paradox, parallel structure, rhythm, visual imagery, melodic combinations, reverse structure, unusual adjectives/adverbs, sense of humor, philosophical bent (Piirto, 1999, p. 241).

Creative Area

Gifted and talented students produce many ideas that are different from the norm, whether "to self, others, a situation, a point in time, a field of study, a cultural group, or a combination of these" (Coleman & Cross, 2001, p. 241). These are the common characteristics that define the creative student:

- has in-depth foundational knowledge;
- prefers complexity and open-endedness;
- contributes new concepts, methods, products, and/or performances;
- has extreme fluency of thoughts and a large number of ideas;
- is observant and pays attention to detail;
- uses unique solutions to problems and improvises;
- challenges existing ideas and/or products;
- connects disparate ideas;
- is constantly asking questions;
- criticizes constructively;
- is a risk taker and is confident;
- is attracted to the novel, complex, and mysterious;
- is a nonconformist, uninhibited in expression, adventurous, and able to resist group pressure;
- accepts disorder;
- tolerates ambiguity—delays closure;
- is persistent and task-committed in areas of interest;
- has a sense of humor;
- is intellectually playful;
- is aware of his or her own creativity;

- is emotionally sensitive—sensitive to beauty;
- is intuitive;
- enjoys time alone; and
- is reflective about the personal creative process (Clark, 1997; Coleman & Cross, 2001; Gardner, 1993; Gilliam et al., 1996; Goertzel & Goertzel, 1962; Gruber, 1982; Guilford, 1950; Khatena, 1992; Perkins, 1981; Piirto, 1999; Renzulli et al., 2002; Ryser & McConnell, 2004; Sternberg, 1988; Tannenbaum, 1983; Torrance, 1974).

Artistic Area

Students who are artistic may demonstrate their abilities in one or more artistic fields such as art, drama, or music. Following are the characteristics an artistically gifted student may exhibit:

General (demonstrated within artistic area)
- chooses artistic activity for projects or during free time;
- studies or practices artistic talent without being told;
- strives to improve his or her artistic skills;
- demonstrates talent for an extended period of time;
- concentrates for long periods of time on artistic projects;
- seems to pick up skills in the arts with little or no instruction;
- possesses high sensory sensitivity;
- observes and shows interest in others who are proficient in the artistic skill;
- uses the artistic area to communicate;
- experiments in the artistic medium;
- sets high standards in the artistic area; and
- demonstrates confidence in the artistic area.

Art
- scribbles earlier than most;
- initiates drawing;

- incorporates large numbers of elements into artwork;
- provides balance and order in artwork;
- elaborates on ideas from other people as a starting point;
- observes details in environment, artistic area;
- has unique, unusual solutions to artistic problems;
- uses unusual and interesting visual imagery;
- is innovative in selecting and using art materials;
- has a highly developed sense of movement and rhythm in drawings;
- has a great feel for color;
- varies the organization of elements to suit different situations;
- uses content that is interesting, tells a story, and/or expresses feelings; and
- produces many drawings.

Drama
- is innovative and creative in performing;
- easily tells a story or gives an account of some experience;
- uses gestures or facial expressions to communicate feelings;
- is adept at role-playing, improvising, and acting out situations;
- identifies with moods and motivations of characters;
- handles body with ease and poise;
- creates original plays or makes up plays from stories;
- commands and holds the attention of a group when speaking;
- evokes emotional responses from listeners;
- communicates feelings by nonverbal means; and
- imitates others—uses voice to reflect changes of idea and mood.

Music

- discriminates fine differences in tone, relative or absolute pitch;
- identifies a variety of sounds (background noise, singers, orchestral instruments);
- varies loudness and softness;
- remembers melodies and can produce them accurately;
- plays an instrument or indicates a strong desire;
- is sensitive to rhythm and changes body movements to tempo;
- dances to tunes with different rhythms;
- can complete a melody;
- creates own melodies;
- likes listening to music; and
- likes producing music with others (Clark & Zimmerman, 1984; Gilliam et al., 1996; Renzulli et al., 2002; Khatena, 1988; 1992; Piirto, 1999; Seashore, Leavis, & Saetveit, 1960; Ryser & McConnell, 2004).

Leadership

Leadership emerges from the situation and is dependent upon variables such as the personality of the leader, status within the group, achievement, intelligence, and the characteristics of the followers. A student with strong leadership skills often has these characteristics:

- is well organized;
- can do backwards planning;
- is visionary—has a holistic view;
- is a problem finder;
- is able to see problems from multiple perspectives;
- is adaptable to new situations;
- can manipulate systems;
- is highly responsible and can be counted on;
- maintains on-task focus;

- is self-confident;
- is a persuasive communicator;
- has a cooperative attitude—works well in groups;
- participates in most social activities and enjoys being around other people;
- influences the behavior of others and is recognized as a leader by peers;
- is respected and/or liked by others;
- is aware of verbal and nonverbal cues—has sophisticated interpersonal skills;
- is emotionally stable; and
- is willing to take risks (Davis & Rimm, 1994; Karnes, 1991; Khatena, 1992; Renzulli et al., 2002).

Affective

A gifted and talented student frequently exhibits these specific affective characteristics:

- is motivated in work that excites;
- persists in completing tasks in areas of interest;
- is self-directed and independent;
- evaluates and judges critically;
- has a high degree of concentration;
- becomes bored with routine tasks;
- is interested in "adult" problems;
- is concerned about right and wrong;
- has a higher self-concept, particularly in academics;
- has high expectations of self and others;
- has a sense of humor;
- is highly sensitive;
- takes other perspectives—is empathic; and
- is a perfectionist (Clark, 1997; Colangelo & Davis, 1991; Coleman & Cross, 2001; Khatena, 1992; Piirto, 1999; Rogers, 2001; Sternberg & Davidson, 1986; Swassing, 1985; Tannenbaum, 1983).

These lists of characteristics may be modified depending on their interaction with other factors such as the school task, the social situation, family background, and individual genetic traits (Clark, 1997; Whitmore, 1980). This interaction often produces groups of students who are not stereotypical of the gifted and talented, particularly in the scientific fields. Such students include those from lower income brackets or different cultural backgrounds, those with disabilities, and females. The identification committee will want to plan a comprehensive program not only to address the diversity within and across gifted and talented students, but also to improve the number of gifted and talented students from underrepresented groups.

Program Options

Ideally, programs should be designed based on the characteristics of the identified students. Most often, however, programs are designed based on state requirements (if they exist) or interested teachers. The program then dictates which students will be served in a specific school, rather than the students' characteristics dictating the nature of the program. Given the national emphasis on academics, the most likely candidates for current programs will be students who have gifts and talents in general intellectual ability or specific academic fields. The long-term goal for districts should be to develop program options that match student characteristics in all of the areas listed in the federal definition.

To provide for accelerated students, those who learn at a faster pace than expected, Southern and Jones (2004) described 18 different types of acceleration, from Advanced Placement classes, credit by examination, concurrent or dual-enrollment classes, and correspondence courses at the secondary level, to continuous progress, subject-matter acceleration, self-paced instruction, and grade skipping at the elementary level. Early admission is also an option at all grade levels from kindergarten to college. With the emphasis on achievement, administrators will be pleased to know that bright students almost always benefit from accelerated programs, gaining approximately one grade-equivalent above the scores of bright, nonaccelerated students (Kulik, 2004). In fact, the research support for acceleration is uniformly positive (Colangelo, Assouline, & Gross, 2004). Students who are challenged are less likely to become unmotivated and are more likely to find friends among intellectual peers.

Different types of courses and curricula may be required for students who have talents in leadership, artistic, and creative areas. Enrichment options might include mentoring, internships, special-topic courses, creative problem solving, independent studies, group seminars, interdisciplinary courses, Super Saturdays, summer school or university courses, and competitions such as Destination Imagination, Odyssey of the Mind, and Future Problem Solving. Mentoring is also frequently described as an important option for developing a novice's talents (Arnold & Subotnik, 1995).

Each of the students described previously will require different programming options. James will need to be accelerated to learn new concepts in math and reading either within the same classroom or across grade levels. He will also need a teacher to guide him in studying his passion area, black holes. While James is gifted in those areas that are most often provided by schools, the other students are not. For example, LaTasha is fortunate in being able to develop her musical talent through private lessons, but others with artistic talents might not have the necessary resources and would benefit from a within-school program beginning at the elementary level. Brandon is also more interested in engineering a new rocket than in the traditional core subject areas of reading, math, science, and social studies. His teacher or a teacher trained in gifted and talented education will need to integrate his interests within the math and science areas or perhaps develop a special independent study where he would work with a mentor. Amanda might also benefit from a mentor, an individual who is in a leadership position within the community. This mentor would be able to help her learn more about community networks, creating new visions, and organizing groups. For more information about developing standards, the reader may be interested in the National Association for Gifted Children's book, *Aiming for Excellence: Annotations to the NAGC Pre-K–Grade 12 Gifted Program Standards* (Landrum, Callahan, & Shaklee, 2001).

Summary

A school district will want to design a variety of program options to match the characteristics of identified gifted students. These students will vary within and across the defined areas of giftedness: general intellectual ability, specific academic fields, leadership, creativity, and the arts. Their potential may not be realized without an environment that facilitates and nurtures their gifts.

Identifying Characteristics of Gifted and Talented Students and Program Options: Decisions to Be Made

1. What are the characteristics of gifted students in the school?
2. How do these characteristics match the areas of giftedness as defined by the state's definition? The federal definition?
3. What program options will be available to serve students with those characteristics?
4. What are the human and material resources that will be needed to offer these program options?

Selecting Multiple Assessments

The identification committee will want to select assessments that match the areas of giftedness, the school district's program options, or both. For example, if a school district will be serving students who are gifted in the academic areas of math, science, social studies, and English/language arts, then assessments will need to be identified that align with each of these academic areas. Similar alignments would need to be made for other areas of giftedness such as leadership, creativity, the arts, and general intellectual ability. For instance, achievement tests would not be as appropriate as an audition for students who have talents in drama. For any of these areas, the identification committee will want to select more than one assessment.

Multiple assessments are important because (a) a single test cannot sample all of the behaviors that might be exhibited in a particular area of talent, (b) scores vary across assessments, and (c) a variety of sources (e.g., parents, teachers, students, peers) will provide a broader picture of the student (Coleman & Cross, 2001; Johnsen, 2004c; Salvia & Ysseldyke, 2001). Assessments may include quantitative instruments such as achievement, aptitude, and intelligence tests and/or qualitative instruments such as portfolios, interviews, observations, and checklists. Quantitative instruments assign numbers in comparing students with one another, while qualitative instruments use words to describe an individual student's strengths (Ryser, 2004). In selecting qualitative or quantitative assessments, educators need to consider these questions (Jolly & Hall, 2004):

1. *What is the age of the assessment?* The age of the instrument is based on the date when the norms were collected. An assessment that is more than 12 years old should not be used because of the changing demographics of the United States.

2. *What is the purpose for the assessment?* The assessment should relate to the area of giftedness, to the identification of gifted and talented students, and to the program option. For example, an achievement test would not be an appropriate measure to use for identifying students who are talented in the visual arts. Instead, an art student might show his or her best work in a portfolio.

3. *Is the assessment valid for the purpose?* The technical manual should provide validity studies that show how the assessment samples the domain, how well it relates to other similar assessments, and how well it predicts membership in a group or performance in the classroom. For the purpose of identification, educators will want to know if the assessment is able to discriminate gifted from nongifted students in the domain of interest.

4. *Is the assessment nonbiased?* Bias may enter the identification process at a variety of points. Nominators may have negative attitudes toward certain groups of students, exclusive definitions, or tests that are not fair to students from lower income or linguistically different

backgrounds (Frasier, 1997; Ryser, 2004). Test fairness may be improved by (a) having norms that are representative of minority groups, (b) limiting language requirements for linguistically different students (e.g., using nonverbal assessments), and (c) examining each item for bias either with experts or statistically.

5. *Is the assessment reliable?* The technical manual should provide reliability studies to show that the assessment consistently measures the domain (e.g., internal consistency), is consistent over time (e.g., test-retest reliability), and is consistent between raters or observers (e.g., interrater/scorer reliability). Reliability is an important concept for both quantitative and qualitative assessments. For this reason, those who score portfolios or those who complete checklists need to be trained to ensure consistency across students, classrooms, and schools.

6. *Do the norms match national census data and reflect the school district's population?* For norm-referenced tests, the authors should provide a table that shows the percentage of students in each of the norming groups (e.g., male vs. female) and how these percentages relate to the national census data. If the school varies considerably from the national norms, the district may want to consider local norms for meaningful comparisons.

7. *What types of scores does the instrument provide?* Tests provide a variety of scores, including raw scores, percentile ranks, grade-equivalent scores, and standard scores. When using multiple assessments, standard scores are essential for comparison purposes.

8. *How is the test administered?* If the test is to be used for screening a large number of students, the administrator

may want to consider a group-administered test. If students are referred for assessment, either individual or group administered formats are acceptable. Another important facet to consider is the degree of training required to administer the assessment. For example, only school psychologists may administer some tests such as the Wechsler Intelligence Scale for Children, Fourth Edition (WISC-IV). Some qualitative assessments such as portfolios require more professional development. In any case, all who are involved in the administration of assessments should have training and be aware of the American Psychological Association Guidelines (see http://www.apa.org/ethics).

9. *What is the cost of administering the assessment?* Once strong assessments have been identified, administrators will want to consider costs in terms of both human and material resources. How much does the assessment cost? How much training is needed? How long does it take to administer the assessment?

A number of resources are available that review instruments. These include the *Buros Mental Measurements Yearbooks* (Buros Center for Testing, n.d.); *Test Critiques, Volumes I–X* (Keyser & Sweetland, 2004); *Tests in Print, Volume VI* (Murphy, Plake, Impara, & Spies, 2002); *Tests: A Comprehensive Reference for Assessments in Psychology, Education, and Business, Fifth Edition* (Maddox, 2004); and Jolly and Hall's (2004) chapter "Technical Information Regarding Assessment," which reviews assessments frequently used in gifted education.

Summary

When selecting instruments, the identification committee will want to review both quantitative and qualitative assessments that match each area of giftedness. Multiple assessments provide a broader, more valid perspective that can only be achieved from varied sources. These assessments need to be selected carefully, with the committee critiquing their technical qualities and their requirements for human and material resources.

Selecting Multiple Assessments:
Decisions to Be Made

1. What quantitative assessments match the area of giftedness and the school district's program option?
2. What qualitative assessments match the area of giftedness and the school district's program option?
3. Are a variety of sources used?
4. Are the assessments technically adequate?
5. Does the district have the material and human resources to administer this set of assessments?

Once the identification committee has identified areas of giftedness that will be served in a variety of program options and
selected an array of assessments for each of these areas and programs, they are ready to develop an identification procedure.
The procedure should be aligned with state requirements, and
it should address equal access concerns according to Title VI
guidelines of the Civil Rights Act of 1964.

Phases of the Identification Procedure

Generally, an identification procedure includes three
phases: (1) nomination, (2) screening, and (3) selection. In those
states where gifted and talented falls under special education leg-
islation, a prereferral phase may also be added to the procedure.

Nomination

During this phase, nominations are solicited from a variety
of sources: teachers, parents, peers, counselors, psychologists,
administrators, community members, and the student. The

main purpose of this phase is to ensure that all students who might have potential in the areas that are served by the district are nominated. Particular attention needs to be given to special groups such as students with disabilities, who are from minority or lower income backgrounds, who have limited English proficiency, or are from rurally isolated areas. Professional development for administrators and teachers and orientations for parents and other interested community members are key elements in the process. Research suggests that teachers identify more children when trained (Gear, 1978) and that parents are better than teachers in identifying very young gifted children (Jacobs, 1971).

A prereferral phase may enhance the number of students who are nominated by teachers. This type of assessment might be described as "dynamic." Dynamic models include an element of assessing baseline abilities, teaching, and reassessing (Borland & Wright, 1994). For example, a teacher might design tasks that require problem solving or complex strategies, observe how students perform, and then have the students reflect on their performance. In this way, the teacher might discover gifted students who not only have a greater knowledge base, but also are better at applying this knowledge (Johnsen, 1997). Teachers might also systematically vary the pacing and types of tasks and observe the students' responses in the classroom. For example, how might students react to long-range assignments in their interest areas? If allowed to pace themselves, how quickly do students learn new concepts? When given choices of alternative activities, what types of tasks do students select?

At the end of the nomination phase, the school should have a large pool of applicants, approximately 25–30%, who will proceed to the second phase of identification, which is screening. Movement to the next phase should not be based on a single criterion, such as a teacher nomination, but on multiple sources of information.

Screening

During this phase, specific assessment instruments will be administered that match the gifted program area. For example, intelligence tests might be administered to identify students who have abilities in the general intellectual area, systematic observations of teamwork for students with talents in leadership, and portfolios might be collected for students with talents in the arts, creative and productive thinking, or specific academic areas. Some assessments such as portfolios or intelligence tests may be used across multiple areas, while others will be specific to a single area (e.g., an audition in the performing arts).

Assessments during the screening phase need to match not only the area of giftedness, but also the characteristics of the students. If a student is not fluent in English, nonverbal assessments need to be used. All students should have an opportunity to demonstrate their best performance.

Selection

A committee of at least three professionals who have training in gifted education will meet to select those students who will benefit from the program options. All data from the nomination and screening phases should be considered. Initially, the committee may want to identify students by number only to ensure objectivity, with anecdotal information added later.

The number of identified students will likely vary from year to year. Some years, for example, there may be more students talented in mathematics than in other years. The district will want to create program options that are flexible and match those students who need services not normally provided in the general education classroom. The committee may also want to create a differentiation plan that is based on each student's strengths and weaknesses that includes long- and short-term goals, classroom activities within the gifted and general education program, and evaluation.

Appeals and Due Process

If parents dispute the appropriateness of a placement or program decision regarding their child, they have a right to appeal the decision using due process procedures in some states. Due process procedures are imposed on school districts under the 5th and 14th amendments (Karnes & Marquardt, 1991). To assure these rights, school districts need to establish a process that includes a sequence of steps and time frames that progress from a local appeal to a state or even federal appeal. These steps might include (1) an initial parent meeting with the local selection committee, (2) a parent meeting with the school district committee that would include the director of the gifted program, and (3) a presentation to the board of trustees. If none of the meetings at the district level resolve the issues, then the district may want to involve an impartial, professional mediator. If mediation is unsuccessful, then the parents or the school district may want to contact the state education agency and initiate a formal hearing. At the state level, both sides may have counsel and present expert witnesses. Finally, if none of these steps resolve the conflict, the parents, the school district, or both may want to litigate in state or federal courts.

Equal Access

Equal access means that, at each phase of the identification process, students have the same opportunity to be nominated, screened, and selected. The Office for Civil Rights has developed a checklist to provide an overview of access concerns related to school districts' gifted programs (Trice & Shannon, 2002).

Statistical Analysis

Determine if minority students are statistically underrepresented in gifted programs. A statistically significant underrepresentation of minority students warrants a further,

school-by-school inquiry including statistical data/analyses regarding:

- racial/ethnic composition (%) of the district's student enrollment;

- racial/ethnic composition (%) of student population receiving gifted services;

- number of students by race/ethnicity referred for evaluation for gifted eligibility;

- number of students by race/ethnicity determined eligible for gifted services; and

- number of students by race/ethnicity withdrawing from, or otherwise discontinuing participation in, gifted programs/services.

Notice

Is the notice of the gifted program, with respect to both content and method of dissemination, effective?

- Notice simply and clearly explains the purpose of the program, referral/screening procedures, and eligibility criteria and identifies the district's contact person.

- Notice is provided annually to students, parents, and guardians in a manner designed to reach all segments of the school community.

Referral/Screening

Are referral/screening practices and procedures applied in a nondiscriminatory manner and do the district's practices and procedures provide equal access for all qualified students so that no disparity exists in referral rates of minority students?

- Multiple alternative referral sources (e.g., teachers, parents, etc.) are, in practice, accessible to and utilized by all segments of the school community.

- Teachers and other district staff involved in the referral process have been trained or provided guidance regarding the characteristics of both giftedness in general and in special populations.

- Referral or screening criteria are applied in a nondiscriminatory manner.

- All referral criteria or screening guidelines are directly related to the purpose of the gifted program.

- Standardized tests *and* cutoff scores are appropriate (valid and reliable) for the purpose of screening students for gifted services.

Evaluation/Placement

Are eligibility criteria and procedures applied in a nondiscriminatory manner and do they ensure equal access for all qualified students?

- Eligibility criteria are applied in a nondiscriminatory manner.

- Eligibility criteria are consistent with the purpose and implementation of the gifted program:

  - Eligibility is based on multiple criteria.
  - Criteria include multiple assessment measures.
  - Eligibility incorporates component test scores as appropriate.

- Assessment instruments/measures and cutoff scores are appropriate (valid and reliable) for the purpose of identifying students for gifted services.

- To the extent that subjective assessment criteria are utilized, those individuals conducting the assessments have been provided guidelines and training to ensure proper evaluations.

- Alternative assessment instruments are utilized in appropriate circumstances.

- If private testing is permitted as the basis for an eligibility determination, it does not have a disparate impact on minority students. If it does, the use of such testing is legitimately related to the successful implementation of the program and is used only because no less-discriminatory alternative exists that would achieve the same objective.

Program Participation

Are continued eligibility standards/criteria and procedures applied in a nondiscriminatory manner, and do they ensure equal access for all qualified students?

- Continued eligibility standards/criteria are applied in a nondiscriminatory manner.

- Continued eligibility standards/criteria are consistent with the purpose and implementation of the gifted program.

- Implementation procedures and practices facilitate equal access for all students.

Summary

The identification procedure is comprised of three phases: (1) nomination, (2) screening, and (3) selection. During nomination, multiple sources provide information about specific students. Sometimes, a prereferral phase that involves assessing baseline abilities, teaching, and reassessing is added during the nomination phase. This dynamic approach allows students opportunities to demonstrate their ability in learning and applying knowledge. Nominated students are then assessed further during the screening phase with quantitative and qualitative instruments. Finally, a committee of at least three people selects students who will profit from the gifted program options. Disagreements involving the identification process may be resolved through a due process procedure that the district outlines. In all stages, the identification committee will want to ensure equal access for all groups of students.

Developing an Identification Procedure That Ensures Equal Access: Decisions to Be Made

1. What phases will be included in the identification procedure?
2. What assessments will be used during each phase?
3. Who will serve on the selection committee? How will they be trained?
4. What due process procedures will be initiated?
5. How will equal access be ensured throughout all phases?

Implementing the Identification Procedure

The identification committee has four tasks to accomplish during the implementation stage:

- secure administrators and then approval from the board of trustees;

- provide professional development for administrators and teachers;

- provide an orientation for parents and interested community members; and

- administer assessments.

Approval

At this stage, approval should be assured if the identification committee has involved important stakeholders throughout the planning process. Administrators, particularly principals, will need to examine the final draft before the committee submits written policies to the board of trustees for approval. Any expressed concerns can be addressed at this time, particularly in the area of human and material resources. For example, when will the identification process begin? When will the data be collected for each of the assessments? Who will be involved in the collection and organization of the data? How much professional development will be required? Who will conduct the professional development and who will participate in it? What time will be provided for participation? What budget will pay for the assessments?

Once the essential issues are resolved, the committee will then present the written policies to the board of trustees. These policies will need to include (a) the state or district's definition of gifted and talented; (b) procedures and forms for each phase of assessment (nomination, screening, and selection); (c) provisions regarding reassessment; (d) procedures for exiting students from the program; (e) handling of transfer students; and (f) the appeals process. (Some of these forms are included in the Appendix.)

Professional Development

Everyone involved in the identification of gifted students must have professional development in at least the nature and needs of gifted students, instructional strategies, and program options. This overview can be enhanced through the use of concrete examples in which teachers actually observe gifted students' performance in the classroom using dynamic assessment. In addition, training of teachers and other professionals who will be collecting data or administering specific assessment instruments must be provided to ensure reliability and validity. The assessment standards of the American Psychological Association should be distributed so that everyone is aware of informed consent, confidentiality, and the importance of a standardized process for administering and interpreting qualitative and quantitative assessments (American Psychological Association, 2003).

Qualitative assessments often require more training than quantitative assessments because directions for collecting information are not always standardized. For example, with portfolios, how will students and parents be informed about the collection of data? What will the teacher say when introducing the portfolio? Who will collect the evidence for the portfolio? Will there be any standardized lessons across classrooms? When and how often will data be collected? How will confidentiality be maintained throughout the process? What criteria will be used for including items in the portfolio? (For a discussion of portfolios, see Johnsen & Ryser, 1997, and Texas Education Agency, n. d.)

Nationally normed tests tend to have specific administration directions in their manuals. Those administering these tests should have the necessary training in educational and psychological measurements and follow the directions explicitly. It is helpful for those who are administering quantitative instruments to have some time to practice using the test with others. If the same procedures and processes are used consistently across schools, then the district will have some assurance that all students have an equal opportunity of being identified.

Orientation

Orientations for parents, guardians, and other interested community members should occur on a regular basis, such as on parents' night or an open house at the school, so that all parents have an opportunity to learn about the gifted and talented program and the identification process—particularly the nomination phase. Parents and guardians are an excellent source of information because children don't always perform similarly at school as they do at home. Parents and guardians often have more opportunities to observe their child's interests, collections, hobbies, friends, and talents than teachers do. For example, a child's interest in peregrine falcons or emperor penguins may not be a part of the curriculum, but his or her bedroom is full of pictures and books that describe this passion. Parents and guardians need to know what characteristics to observe and how these characteristics will be served in programs for gifted and talented students. In this way, they will understand the purpose for this qualitatively different education and be better collaborators in the identification process.

If parents and guardians are involved in the collection of any information, they will need specific directions about the assessments they will be using. If they are completing observation checklists, the forms should not contain educational jargon or require extensive writing abilities that might prohibit some parents from completing them. These forms should be available to all parents in their primary language. Teachers may also need to make individual contacts with parents who are not as actively involved in the school. To increase participation during the nomination phase, districts may even want to consider placing information about the identification process in the district newsletter or hometown newspaper.

Administering Assessments

Once orientations and professional development have been completed, the administration of all of the assessments should flow easily. A schoolwide calendar needs to be developed that describes when assessments should be distributed and collected (see Table 1). A person at each school or at each grade level will need to coordinate the dissemination and collection of assessments and information to ensure the integrity of the process. Any screening that is an addition to the general education program and is intended for identification for a special program requires parental permission.

Table 1
School Calendar

Aug. 25–31	Schedule professional development and orientations. Use the appropriate PowerPoint presentations for teachers, administrator, and parent groups.
Sept. 1	Nominations begin. Distribute teacher and parent inventories. Send flyers home with students. Make sure that all students are considered. Remember special education students.
Sept. 30	Collect all of the nomination forms.
Oct. 1	Have gifted teacher orient students to the process of collecting evidence for the portfolio. Send letter to parents about collecting portfolio evidence.
All of Oct.	Have teachers, students, and parents collect portfolio items.
Oct. 30	Complete collection of portfolio evidence.
Nov. 15	Have identification committee meet to consider students who will be tested further. Send permission letters to parents requesting additional testing.
Nov. 15–30	Administer formal assessments during this 2-week period.
Dec. 1–7	Organize identification information for the selection committee.
Dec. 8–16	The committee meets to select students for different program options.
Dec. 17	Letters are sent to parents and teachers about students who are selected for the program.
Jan. 15	Appeals are due to the campus coordinator.
Jan. 22	Appeals are considered by the committee.
Jan. 23	Notify parents by letter if the appeal was granted or not.

Summary

Important stakeholders and the board of trustees need to approve the identification procedures and policies before implementation begins. Once approval has occurred, professional staff and all individuals who are involved in identifying gifted and talented students, including parents, will need to be trained in the nature and needs of gifted students and specific methods for gathering information. Training is particularly important for administering qualitative instruments to ensure reliability and validity. Once approval and professional development has occurred, the coordinator of programs for the gifted and talented develops a calendar to protect the integrity of the process.

Implementing the Identification Procedure: Decisions to Be Made

1. Have the identification policies been approved by the Board of Trustees and important stakeholders?
2. Have the educators who are involved in the identification process received professional development?
3. Have parents and guardians received an overview of the characteristics of gifted students, the identification process, and program options?
4. Has a coordinator of assessment been appointed at each campus or grade level?
5. Has a districtwide calendar been developed?

When the data have been collected at the nomination and/or screening process, the identification committee will need to meet to organize the information, interpret the results, and select students for either movement to the next phase in the process (i.e., from nomination to screening) or for various program options.

Organizing Information

Information from qualitative and quantitative assessments may be organized in a variety of ways, including case studies, profiles, and matrices. These forms need to meet the following guidelines to ensure technical adequacy (Johnsen, 2004c):

Guideline 1:
Each assessment should have equal value in the decision-making process.
If each of the assessments is reliable and valid for the purpose of identifying gifted and talented students, then each should receive equal weight in the decision-making process.

Review the following examples that show how committees may unintentionally weight some assessments more than others.

Example 1. A committee decides to ignore the parent nomination data in favor of the teacher nomination data because the committee views teacher information as more valid than parent information. Unless the school has collected evaluation data that show teacher information is more predictive of performance in the gifted program than parent information, then both sets of data should be considered equally.

Example 2. A committee decides to use a cutoff score on an achievement test (e.g., 85th percentile) as entry into the nomination process. In this case, the achievement test becomes a gate that will exclude any students who have not learned school-acquired information, particularly those from lower income backgrounds. Remember that academic potential may be demonstrated in other ways, such as in dynamic assessments (Borland & Wright, 1994).

Example 3. A committee is more heavily influenced by an intelligence test (a quantitative assessment) than it is by a portfolio of student work (a qualitative assessment). Again, if each of the assessments has equal technical qualities, then both should be considered equally.

Example 4. The teacher rates the portfolio, completes a nomination checklist, and provides grades for the committee's consideration. In this case, a single source, the teacher, is triple-weighted, getting three votes to select a student.

Example 5. On the matrix, each of the subtests from one achievement test receives points. This approach means that a single measure has a multiplied weight. On the other hand, if a test assesses distinctly different areas, such as reasoning versus achievement, then each of the subtests might be considered as providing different types of information. For instance, a student might perform in the superior range on a reasoning subtest, but only in the average range on the achievement subtest.

Guideline 2:
The scores from each assessment should be comparable.

The assessments may produce a variety of different scores (e.g., raw scores, percentiles, stanines, standard scores). Some of these scores can be compared with one another, while others cannot. For example, raw scores can never be compared with one another. This comparison would be similar to comparing grades between two teachers' classrooms. Consequently, raw scores need to be converted to a standard before they may be interpreted. Similarly, percentiles are a rank order of students who took a particular test; however, they may be used if they are based on standard scores. Indeed, standard scores have an advantage over other types of scores because the measurement units are equal and can be averaged or manipulated (Feldhusen, Baska, & Womble, 1981).

Most scores may be converted by using simple formulas (see Johnsen, 2004b, pp. 155–157 for conversion directions). Test manuals and publishers also provide conversion charts that compare various test scores with one another and to a normal distribution (e.g., the bell-shaped curve). Looking at Table 2, a committee may determine that a performance at the 95th percentile is similar to a standard score of 124 (deviation IQ), to a Z-score of 1.6, and to a stanine score of 8, all of which indicate that the student is performing in the superior range.

Besides making sure that the assessment scores are comparable, the committee also needs to know the scores' reference population or norm group. Are the scores from the local school only, from a state sample, or from a national sample? Are they from a sample of students who received nominations from the

Table 2
Relationships of Various Standard Scores to Percentile Ranks and Descriptions

Distance From Mean	Description (% of pop.)	Percentile Ranks	Standard Scores		Stanines (% of pop.)
			Dev. IQ	Z Score	
+3SD		99.9	150.0	3.3	
		99.9	145.0	3.0	
		99.8	143.5	2.9	
		99.7	142.0	2.8	
	Very Superior (2.34%)	99.6	140.5	2.7	
		99.5	140.0	2.7	
		99.5	139.0	2.6	
		99.4	137.5	2.5	
		99.2	136.0	2.4	9 (4%)
		99	135.0	2.3	
		99	134.5	2.3	
		99	133.0	2.2	
		98	131.5	2.1	
+2SD		98	130.0	2.0	
		97	128.5	1.9	
		96	127.0	1.8	
	Superior (6.87%)	96	125.5	1.7	
		96	125.0	1.7	
		95	124.0	1.6	
		93	122.5	1.5	
		92	121.0	1.4	8 (7%)
		91	120.0	1.3	
		90	119.5	1.3	
	Above-Average (16.12%)	88	118.0	1.2	
+1SD		86	116.5	1.1	
		84	115.0	1.0	7 (12%)
		82	113.5	.9	
		79	112.0	.8	
		76	110.5	.7	
	Average (49.51%)	75	110.0	.7	
		73	109.0	.6	
		69	107.5	.5	6 (17%)
		66	106.0	.4	
		63	105.0	.3	
		62	104.5	.3	
		58	103.0	.2	
Mean		54	101.5	.1	
		50	100.0	0	
		46	98.5	-.1	
		42	97.0	-.2	5 (20%)
		38	95.5	-.3	
		37	95.0	-.3	

local school? Are they from a national sample of gifted students or a national sample of general education students?

Different comparison groups will influence scores. For example, Jennifer might perform better when compared to a school sample that includes all students, rather than to a sample that includes only nominated students. Similarly, she would perform better if she were compared to all students in a national sample, rather than only to gifted students in a national sample. Young kindergarten children may also appear to do less well than older children from the same grade level. Therefore, in making decisions, the committee needs to consider the variety of scores and the reference groups for each assessment.

Guideline 3:
Each assessment's standard error of measurement must be considered.

The selection committee needs to remember that an assessment is simply an estimate of a student's performance at a particular time. Every assessment contains a certain amount of error based on its reliability or consistency. The more reliable the instrument, the less error it will include. Even nationally normed assessments may have a standard error of measurement (SEM) of five points. This amount of error means that a student's score may actually range from the very superior level to the average level within one measure or across measures.

For example, let's consider Jay, a student who scored 130 on an intelligence test with an SEM of five points. Using Table 3, which shows the confidence levels and standard errors of measurement, the selection committee might be sure that Jay will perform between 125 and 135 on this test 68% of the time (i.e., the committee is adding and subtracting one SEM from the score of 130). They might be sure that Jay will perform between 120 and 140 on this test 95% of the time (i.e., the committee is now adding and subtracting two SEMs from the score of 130). They might be even surer that Jay will perform between 118 and 143 on this test 99% of the time (i.e., the committee is now adding and subtracting 2.6 SEMs from the score of 130). As can be seen with this example, a test score actually lies somewhere within a range of scores that is established by the standard error of measurement. In this case, Jay is performing within the above-average to very superior ranges (see Table 3). While most test manuals include the SEM for each age and grade level, this error may be calculated for any assessment (see Johnsen, 2004b, pp. 159–163 for directions). In all cases, the selection committee will want to organize their data in a manner that incorporates the error in each of the assessments.

Table 3
Confidence Levels
for Different Standard Errors
of Measurement

Confidence Level	Band of Error
68%	± 1 SEM
85%	± 1.44 SEMs
90%	± 1.645 SEMs
95%	± 1.96 SEMs
99%	± 2.576 SEMs

Guideline 4:
The best score indicates a student's potential.

When organizing data, the committee should consider a student's best performance. Compressing the data into a single score or number may be misleading and conceal a student's potential, particularly when there is a great deal of variability in performance.

For example, Zack's scores range from the average (e.g., achievement) to the very superior ranges (e.g., portfolio evidence). In his case, the classroom evidence (e.g., the portfolio) may be more indicative of Zack's potential than a standardized achievement test. The highest score is most often the truest (Tolan, 1992a, 1992b).

Guideline 5:
Students should be described with more than numbers.

The selection committee must have access to information that also describes the student's performance so that a complete picture of the student may be portrayed. This information may be provided through parent or teacher anecdotes, student interviews, evidence from the portfolio, or clinical observations. These descriptions become critical when selecting a program option that matches the student's characteristics.

Forms

A variety of forms are being used to summarize assessment information. Pretend that selection committees are now meeting to review applicants for the gifted programs in different school districts. While the forms used to organize data vary from school to school, they all meet the previous criteria for organizing data.

In summary, the committee will want to follow these guidelines in using forms that organize data:

1. Are assessments weighted equally?

2. Are the scores comparable?

3. Are errors in measures considered?

4. Is the student's best performance visible?

5. Is there a qualitative description of the student's performance?

School District 1 (Case Study Approach)
On the next page is a set of data that the selection committee has received regarding a nominated third-grade student, Javier (see Figure 1). The district considers students for their gifted program if they perform in the superior ranges on qualitative and quantitative assessments. Javier has performed in the superior to very superior ranges on the aptitude indicators, scoring 130 on the Screening Assessment for Gifted Elementary

Student: Javier
ID #: 97-4253
D.O.B.: Oct. 31, 1997

Home School/Grade: Spring/Grade 3
Date of Review: March 18, 2006

I. Nomination

	Standard	Score Obtained	Comments
Parents	95th percentile SS 124	(Yes)/ No	building rocket
Counselor	91st percentile SS120	(Yes)/ No	(see interview)
Teacher	84th percentile SS 115	Yes /(No)	concern-achieve

Achievement–Iowa Test of Basic Skills

	Standard	Score Obtained	Comments
Reading	84th percentile SS 113.5	Yes /(No)	above average
Math	90th percentile SS 121	(Yes)/ No	above average
Science	93rd percentile SS 122.5	(Yes)/ No	superior range
Social Studies	82nd percentile SS 113.5	Yes /(No)	above average

II. Screening committee recommendation (signatures on back)

The Screening Committee has reviewed this student's data and has determined that he/she:
✔ Is recommended for additional screening.
__ Is recommended and an exception is made because _____.
__ Is not recommended for additional screening.

III. Screening

	Standard	Score Obtained	Comments
Interview	Exhibits characteristics	(Yes)/ No	see notebook
Tests Administered			
SAGES-2	98th percentile SS 130	(Yes)/ No	high reasoning
TONI-3	99th percentile SS 135	(Yes)/ No	high reasoning
Portfolio	Exhibits characteristics	(Yes)/ No	see photo of rocket

IV. Selection Committee Recommendation: _____

Figure 1. Case Study Form

Note. Adapted from the Plano ISD identification procedure, 1993.

Students, Second Edition (SAGES-2; Johnsen & Corn, 2001) and 135 on the Test of Nonverbal Intelligence, Third Edition (TONI-3; Brown, Sherbenou, & Johnsen, 1997). The committee rated his portfolio items as indicating the characteristics that are often associated with gifted students. In addition, his parents and the counselor in the school recommended him highly. However, his achievement scores and his teacher recommendation placed him in the above-average range.

Some of the anecdotal information suggested that Javier is particularly interested in science and has been involved in building a rocket prototype at home. Through an interview, the counselor became aware of Javier's interest in science. He shared a notebook of facts about space travel that he had been keeping since the first grade. His teacher, however, was concerned that Javier's work in class was not at the gifted level. She believed that he would fall behind and not be able to pass the state-mandated test if he were accepted into the gifted program. The selection committee therefore had to decide if these data indicated that Javier needed gifted and talented program services.

After discussion, the committee came to the conclusion that Javier has potential and would benefit from a program that focused on his science interests. He would still be able to continue in his general education classes in the core areas of math, reading, and social studies, but would go to the gifted classroom to pursue his science interests. The teacher in the gifted program would assist him in conducting independent research on rockets, and perhaps, as his knowledge base grew, find a mentor for him from the local community college. In the general education program, the committee recommended that the core areas be differentiated for him, particularly in math to see if he might be able to progress at a faster rate that is commensurate with his potential. The committee also wanted to evaluate his progress in the core areas over the next year and determine if more services might be needed.

School District II (Minimum Scores Approach)

This school district generally considers the top 5% for their gifted programs and uses a minimum scores approach to organizing data. For each assessment, the school district has defined a minimum score that is aligned with the 95th percentile, or a 124 standard score. For example, the Wechsler Intelligence Scale for Children, Fourth Edition (WISC-IV; Wechsler, 2003) is used to determine aptitude. With a three-point standard error of measurement, a student would need to have a minimum score of 121 to meet this standard at the 68% confidence level. Using this procedure, a minimum score is determined for each of the other assessments. If a student meets at least three of the minimum standards, he or she is considered for the gifted and talented program.

In Alexandra's case, she met the minimum score on the achievement test, the Scales for Rating the Behavioral Characteristics of Superior Students (Renzulli et al., 2002), and the parent checklist, performing in the superior range. On the other hand, she scored in the above-average range on the aptitude measure (the WISC-IV) and the product portfolio (see Figure 2). Comments indicated that Alexandra enjoyed school and performed well in all of the core academic areas. She received mostly A's and B's on her report card. She appeared to have many friends and was progressing well in the fifth grade. The selection committee had to determine if Alexandra would profit from placement in a program that focuses on specific academic aptitude.

The committee decided that, at that time, Alexandra appeared to be profiting from the general education program, but her activities should be more accelerated to determine if she would be able to advance at a more rapid pace. The committee planned to reexamine Alexandra's progress in several months to see if the gifted program, which is accelerated, would better meet her needs.

Identification Number: 6783   **Recommended for Placement:** (Yes) No
Name: Alexandra   **Date of Review:** January 31, 2006
Date of Birth: May 6, 1997   **School:** Jefferson
Parents/Guardian: Jazzmine   **Teacher/Grade:** Robinson / Grade 4
Address: 325 Holiday, #5
Phone: 678-3921 (H); 698-1209 (W)

Instruments	SEM	Minimum Score	Actual Score	+/-	Comments
Aptitude (WISC IV)	3	121	119 90th percentile	-	Stronger in areas requiring acquired knowledge
Achievement (CAT)	5	119	130 98th percentile	+	Strong in all areas
Motivation (Renzulli)	5	119	124 95th percentile	+	Makes all A's and B's
Parent (Checklist)	4	120	127 96th percentile	+	Alex does her homework right away
Products	4	120	115 84th percentile	-	Not many original ideas

Comments:
Alexandra enjoys school and performs well in all of the core academic areas. She is well adjusted socially and has many friends.

Figure 2. Minimum Scores Form

School District III (Profile Approach)

This school district has chosen to display its data using a profile (see Figure 3). In this district, they have decided to select the top 10% for the program that focuses on specific academic aptitude. In this way the standard error of measurement

Name: James **ID#:** 6783 **School:** Washington **Teacher:** Shiu	SS 70 85 100 115 130 135 160
Grade: 7 **D.O.B:** 5/6/95 **Parents:** George and Diane **Address:** 424 Overview Ln.	% 0 2 8 16 25 50 70 84 91 98 99.9
Phone: 741-9840 (H); 741-4563 (W) **Date of Review:** 1/31/06	SS -2sd -1sd M +1sd +2sd +3sd +4sd

	-2sd	-1sd	M	+1sd	+2sd	+3sd	+4sd
1. Product/Performance Raw score: 6/8 points SS: 121 (92nd percentile)					•		
2. Teacher Checklist SIGS SS: 124 (95th percentile)					•		
3. Parent Checklist SIGS SS: 121 (92nd percentile)					•		
4. SAT Reading (SS 124; 95th percentile) Mathematics (SS 115; 84th percentile) Science (SS 110; 75th percentile) Social Science (SS 115; 84th percentile)				• • • •			
5. Intelligence Test SAGES-2 Reasoning (SS 135) Math/Science (SS 118) Language/Social Studies (SS 133)				•	•	• •	

Comments and Recommendation:
While James does not make all A's and B's, he is a creative writer (see attached writing samples).

Figure 3. Profile Form

Note. Adapted from the gifted and talented program, Lubbock Independent School District, 1989.

would be integrated into a more inclusive percentage. For example, a standard score of 120 is approximately at the 90th percentile. If a student were to score 120 on an intelligence test that has an SEM of four points, then his or her upper range would be 130, or the top 2%.

Similar to the minimum scores approach, a standard score of 120 is determined for each assessment and listed on the profile form. The student's actual scores are plotted on a graph so that the committee is able to view intraindividual strengths and weaknesses. In this case, the district has plotted all of the subtests on the achievement test; the aptitude test; the subtests on the Scales for Identifying Gifted Students (SIGS; Ryser & McConnell, 2004) checklist, both parent and teacher; and the evidence from the products/performances. Again, the narratives from the teacher, parent, and the student provide additional information for the committee.

The middle school teacher strongly believed that James was a creative writer, and she attached some of his writing samples. James did not make outstanding grades, but he appeared to be able to exert the effort needed to make B's in his classes. His parents seemed to be satisfied with this level of performance. In examining the profile, it is quite clear that James has strengths in the language areas. The committee therefore recommended that James work with a writing mentor in the gifted program and become more involved in the school newspaper. They also recommend that he be placed in a pre-AP (Advanced Placement) class to give him greater opportunities to read more literature and develop his writing abilities.

Summary

While a variety of forms are available to organize assessment information, they need to meet these specific guidelines to ensure their reliability and validity: (a) assessments are equally weighted, (b) scores are comparable, (c) standard error of measurement is considered, (d) intraindividual differences are evident, and (e) students are qualitatively described. Once a technically adequate form is created, the selection committee needs to be trained in the interpretation of the assessments and program options so that each identified student will receive appropriate services.

Organizing Assessment Information, Interpreting Results, and Selecting Students: Decisions to Be Made

1. Has a data organization form been designed that meets these criteria: (a) equal weighted assessments, (b) comparable scores, (c) standard error of measurement, (d) intraindividual differences, and (e) student descriptions?
2. Has the selection committee received professional development in evaluating and interpreting assessment information?
3. Is the selection committee aware of available program options?

Evaluating and Revising Assessment Procedures

The evaluator uses standards to examine the value, quality, usefulness, effectiveness, or significance of what is being evaluated (Johnsen, 2004a). In this case, the school district initiates an evaluation to determine the effectiveness of the procedures for identifying gifted and talented students. While this evaluation may occur internally, the identification committee may decide to select an external evaluator who often brings more credibility and objectivity to the process.

Evaluation Questions

The first step in any evaluation is to identify the key features or questions. Some of these evaluation questions might be selected from state requirements, the Office for Civil Rights, or both. Some of the following questions might be addressed:

1. Are all of the components of the identification procedure being implemented in each phase?

2. Is the implementation occurring consistently across the school district?

3. Does it meet state compliance standards?

4. Are there enough human and material resources to support the identification process?

5. Are all students who might benefit from the program being identified? Do all students have equal access to the program?

6. Do identified students perform successfully in the gifted program?

7. Which assessments are most effective in predicting future performance in the program?

8. Do the assessments relate to one another? Are they assessing different areas of giftedness?

9. Do the assessments discriminate who is talented from who is not talented in a specific program area?

10. Does the population in the district's gifted and talented program reflect the total district population? Are any special groups underrepresented?

11. Have staff who are involved in the identification process received adequate professional development in all phases of the identification procedure?

Given the number of questions that examine an identification procedure, a school district may want to develop a timeline for evaluating different features. For example, during the first year, the school will want to ensure that the identification pro-

cedure is being implemented consistently and that everyone on the staff has been adequately trained. Once these important questions have been addressed, the district may want to determine if the procedures are effective in identifying the students who might benefit from the program.

Data Sources and Instrument Review

Once questions have been identified and a timeline established, the school district will want to identify the types of information that are needed, such as product ratings, performances, anecdotal logs, diaries, identification summary forms from the committees, lesson plans, differentiated units of instruction, observation instruments, interviews, attitude and interest inventories, rating scales, norm-referenced tests, grades, work samples, criterion-referenced tests, school incident reports, questionnaires and surveys, portfolios, and videotapes. Sources of information might be the general education teacher, the gifted and talented teacher, the student's peers, parents, counselors, administrators, school board members, other community members, as well as the student him- or herself.

For instance, in examining how effectively the assessments are predicting performance in the gifted program, the district will want to collect two sets of data: the scores from each of the assessments used in the identification process and a rating of student performance in the classroom (e.g., grades, teacher ratings of expected classroom performances, observations of performance, standardized end-of-course exams, and professional reviews of products). In this example, the school will have already collected much of this information needed for the evaluation, such as the assessment data used during the identification process, but may need to design a new assessment to examine classroom performance. The newly designed instruments will need to be reviewed according to their reliability and validity and field-tested before being distributed school- or districtwide.

Methods

After the assessments and sources of information have been selected for specific questions, the district will need to identify how the information will be collected, how it will be measured, and how it will be described—either quantitatively with numbers or qualitatively with words.

For example, in Table 4, the key question focuses on the "Prediction of Classroom Performance." The types of information collected are the assessments used in the identification process (e.g., teacher nomination, parent nomination, portfolios, achievement tests, and intelligence tests) and the assessments of classroom performance (e.g., teacher ratings, observations, products). The sources of information for each of these assessments are listed in the next column. These sources are varied to provide a complete picture of the student in the classroom. The method then describes how these data were analyzed. Will the data be analyzed using descriptions, examining relationships, or finding differences?

In this case, the main focus will be on identifying the relationships between the assessments used in the identification procedure and performance in the classroom. Some of the performance data will be quantitative, such as the teacher ratings and the product scores, and some will be both quantitative and qualitative, such as the observations. The teacher ratings will be aligned with the program objectives (see Figure 4). The products will be scored using a rubric (see Figure 5), and the observations will examine student engagement, levels of questions, and anecdotal information (see Figure 6).

Data Interpretation

Once the data are collected, quantitative and qualitative analyses need to occur. For quantitative data, the evaluator will use a variety of statistics, and for qualitative data, he or she will examine patterns and themes. Sometimes, simple descriptive statistics are all

Table 4
Types of Information, Source, Method, and Measurement of a Key Question

Key Feature	Type of Information	Source	Method	Assessment
Prediction of Classroom Performance	Achievement and intelligence tests	Student and district	Compare performance on tests to performance in the classroom.	Quantitative
	Parent and teacher nominations	Parent and teacher	Compare performance of students who were nominated to performance in the classroom.	Quantitative
	Portfolios	Student, teacher, and parent	Compare performance on portfolios with performance in the classroom. Describe product-quality differences.	Qualitative and quantitative
	Ratings of classroom performance	Teacher	Relationship between identification assessments and classroom rating; description of performance in the classroom.	Quantitative and qualitative
	Observations of students	Outside evaluator	Relationship between identification assessments, teacher ratings, and observations; description of interactions in the classroom	Quantitative and qualitative
	Classroom Products	Outside evaluator	Relationship between identification assessments, teacher ratings, observations, and products; describe product-quality differences	Quantitative and qualitative

Instructions: The statements below relate to the objectives of the G/T program. Read each of the statements and rate the student according to the degree to which he or she demonstrates these behaviors in your classroom. For example, if you present a problem that requires a solution, does the student "always," "sometimes," "seldom," or "never" come up with an original idea? If the student "always" has original ideas, then you would circle the "4," if "never," then you would circle the "1," and so on. If this behavior is not related to an objective for your classroom, then circle "NA," not applicable.

	Never	Seldom	Sometimes	Always	
1. The G/T student develops creative and productive thinking skills by:					
• Thinking of many ideas	1	2	3	4	NA
• Thinking of varied ideas	1	2	3	4	NA
• Thinking of unusual ideas	1	2	3	4	NA
• Adding to ideas to make better	1	2	3	4	NA
2. The G/T student develops ability to generate original solutions by means of problem solving by:					
• Finding related problems	1	2	3	4	NA
• Finding many original solutions	1	2	3	4	NA
• Generating criteria for selecting solutions	1	2	3	4	NA
• Selling solutions	1	2	3	4	NA
• Implementing solutions	1	2	3	4	NA
3. The G/T student develops oral and written communication skills through verbal and nonverbal activities by:					
• Writing or verbalizing using descriptions	1	2	3	4	NA
• Writing or verbalizing using narratives	1	2	3	4	NA
• Writing or verbalizing using cause/effect	1	2	3	4	NA
• Writing or verbalizing using persuasion	1	2	3	4	NA
4. The G/T student develops and utilizes the independent research process by:					
• Asking questions	1	2	3	4	NA
• Selecting a method of research	1	2	3	4	NA
• Gathering information	1	2	3	4	NA
• Summarizing information	1	2	3	4	NA
• Sharing information	1	2	3	4	NA
5. The G/T student develops leadership and group process skills by:					
• Listening to others' ideas	1	2	3	4	NA
• Expressing ideas	1	2	3	4	NA
• Working cooperatively	1	2	3	4	NA
• Assisting the group in reaching a consensus or making decisions	1	2	3	4	NA
6. The G/T student develops an understanding of his/her own giftedness by:					
• Identifying specialties in self	1	2	3	4	NA
• Identifying specialties in others	1	2	3	4	NA
• Responding to differences	1	2	3	4	NA
• Accepting differences	1	2	3	4	NA
• Valuing differences	1	2	3	4	NA

Figure 4. Teacher rating of student performance

Note. From Johnsen & Ryser, 1997.

Age and developmental appropriateness of product	1 Consistently below grade level	2 Inconsistently below grade level	3 Consistently on grade level	4 Inconsistently above grade level	4 Consistently above grade level
Ability to see relationships and connections	1 Not evidenced	2 Shows some analogies, connections	3 1-2 content areas; representative samples adequately show grade level work	4 1-2 content areas; representative samples adequately show grade level work	4 1-2 content areas; representative samples adequately show above grade level work
Diversity of products	1 1 content area	2 1-2 content areas	3 1-2 content areas; representative samples adequately show grade level	4 1-2 content areas; samples show above level work; critical and creative thinking evidenced	5 3+ content areas; high quality work; above grade level; critical and creative thinking evidenced
Depth of knowledge expressed; demonstrated	1 No in-depth knowledge of topic evidenced	2 Below average knowledge of topic expressed	3 Average knowledge of topic expressed	4 Above average knowledge of topic expressed	5 In-depth knowledge of topic expressed; reader knows topic is a "passion"
Effective use of English language	1 Writings not sequential in order; formats of writing types not followed; poor use of grammar/spelling rules	2 Below average writing skills; weak command of grammar/spelling rules	3 Adequate use of language; able to accomplish task (e.g., a story with all elements); average mistakes in spelling and grammar	4 Some use of figurative language; fluent writing and basically correct grammar and spelling (few mistakes)	5 Multiple use of figurative language (similes, metaphors, idioms, etc.); fluent; concise; correct language

Figure 5. Product rubric

Note. Adapted from Carrollton/Farmers Branch ISD, 1996.

Teacher Questions	Code	R	Student Questions	Code

Record the teacher and student questions verbatim. Indicate in the "R" column if a student response occurred. Code each of the questions by using the categories below.

Codes:
S = Single answer, M = Multiple answer, C = Connections, P = Process,
E = Evaluation/Implications

Figure 6. Levels of questions and student engagement

Note. Adapted from Carrollton/Farmers Branch ISD, 1996.

that are needed; in other cases, more sophisticated statistics might be required. If a school district doesn't have an evaluator who has a strong background in statistics, they might want to collaborate with a university, another school district's research division, or a consultant. In examining the question about the effectiveness of assessments in predicting performance in the gifted program, the observation data, teacher ratings, and portfolio can be quantified by simply using descriptive statistics. During what percentage of time were the students engaged? What percentage of questions was at a higher level of thinking? What was the overall rating for each of the products using professional standards? What rating did each student receive? Qualitatively, the observer might observe how the students responded to the classroom activities and to one another. The most sophisticated statistical procedure will be looking at the ability of the assessments to predict classroom performance (e.g., regression analysis).

Evaluators do need to be cautious in interpreting data, making sure that the sample is representative of the whole. For example, did the observer collect classroom data on more than one day? Did the data represent the majority of the classroom activities? Particularly with observations or other types of qualitative data, the evaluator will want to ask teachers, students, and other participants to verify the information that is recorded so that everyone agrees with the interpretations of the data.

Report

At the conclusion of data collection and interpretation, the evaluator will summarize all of the information that relates to the original question and write a report for those who are interested in the results (e. g., teachers, administrators, school board members, community groups). The report generally has six sections (Johnsen, 2004a):

1. *Executive summary*—provides a synopsis of each of the other sections.

2. *Background information*—provides overall information about the identification procedures in the district.

3. *Purpose of the evaluation*—provides the reason for this study and describes the methods (sample, assessments, and data analysis).

4. *Results*—presents tables, graphs, scores from tests, anecdotal summaries, and other information that addresses the purpose of the evaluation.

5. *Discussion*—relates the results to the original purpose of the study. Were the assessments effective in predicting successful performance in the classroom?

6. *Recommendations*—lists strengths and weaknesses of the district's identification procedures and makes recommendations for changes.

Action

The final step in the evaluation process is for the district to consider the recommendations and decide which ones they are interested in implementing and when.

For example, let's assume that the majority of the assessments are effective in predicting performance in the classroom, but the teacher nomination does not add any new information that is not already a part of the portfolio process. The district will then need to consider if they want to drop this assessment from the array of instruments used during identification or alter the information the teacher provides. Considerations might include the importance of the recommendation to the effectiveness of the identification procedures and to other stakeholders, the cost, and the additional training that might be needed.

Evaluations not only tend to answer some questions, but

also raise others. Their importance is ensuring that every child who has a gift or talent receives services.

Summary

Evaluation is an important aspect of identifying gifted students. It provides the school district with information needed for making the identification procedures more efficient and effective. Steps in the evaluation process include (1) identifying evaluation questions, (2) selecting data sources and instruments, (3) matching the methods with the evaluation questions, (4) interpreting data, (5) writing the report, and (6) implementing the recommendations.

While evaluations may be conducted within the school district, most often schools tend to contract with outside consultants for expertise and to lend more credibility to the process. In all cases, the purpose of evaluations is for improving the overall identification procedure.

Conclusion

School districts that are involved in identifying gifted and talented students need to develop a plan that includes (a) characteristics of gifted and talented students who will be served in
various program options; (b) multiple assessments that match
these characteristics and program options; (c) methods that
ensure equal access across diverse populations; (d) implementation procedures; (e) standards for organizing and interpreting
assessment information; and (e) formative and summative evaluations to improve the overall plan. A well-designed plan is
necessary for the implementation of an effective identification
procedure, one that identifies students who will benefit from
the gifted and talented program.

American Psychological Association (2003). *Ethical principles of psychologists and code of conduct.* Retrieved February 7, 2005, from http://www.apa.org/ethics

Arnold, K. D., & Subotnik, R. F. (1995). Mentoring the gifted: A differentiated model. *Educational Horizons, 73*, 118–123.

Borland, J. H., & Wright, L. (1994). Identifying young, potentially gifted, economically disadvantaged students. *Gifted Child Quarterly, 38*, 164–171.

Brown, L., Sherbenou, R., & Johnsen, S. (1997). *Test of nonverbal intelligence* (3rd ed.). Austin, TX: PRO-ED.

Buros Mental Measurement Yearbooks. (n.d.). Retrieved February 7, 2005, from http://www.unl.edu/buros

Clark, B. (1997). *Growing up gifted: Developing the potential of children at home and at school* (5th ed.). Upper Saddle River, NJ: Merrill.

Clark, G. A., & Zimmerman, E. (1984). *Educating artistically talented students.* Syracuse, NY: Syracuse University Press.

Colangelo, N., & Davis, G. A. (Eds.). (1991). *Handbook of gifted education.* Boston: Allyn and Bacon.

Colangelo, N., Assouline, S. G., & Gross, M. U. M. (2004). *A nation deceived: How schools hold back America's brightest students* (Vol. 1). Iowa City, IA: Connie Belin and Jacqueline N. Blank International Center for Gifted Education and Talent Development.

Coleman, L. J., & Cross, T. L. (2001). *Being gifted in school: An introduction to development, guidance, and teaching.* Waco, TX: Prufrock Press.

Davis, G. A., & Rimm, S. B. (1994). *Education of the gifted and talented* (3rd ed.). Needham Heights, MA: Allyn and Bacon.

Feldhusen, J. F., Baska, L. K., & Womble, S. R. (1981). Using standard scores to synthesize data in identifying the gifted. *Journal for the Education of the Gifted, 4,* 177–185.

Feldhusen, J. F., Hoover, S. M., & Sayler, M. (1989). *Identifying and educating gifted students at the secondary level.* Monroe, NY: Trillium Press.

Frasier, M. M. (1997). Multiple criteria: The mandate and the challenge. *Roeper Review, 20,* 2–4.

Gagné, F. (1995). From giftedness to talent: A developmental model and its impact on the language of the field. *Roeper Review, 18,* 103–111.

Gagné, F. (1999). Gagné's differentiated model of giftedness and talent (DMGT). *Journal for the Education of the Gifted, 22,* 230–234.

Gardner, H. (1993). *Creating minds: An anatomy of creativity seen through the lives of Freud, Einstein, Picasso, Stravinsky, Eliot, Graham, and Gandhi.* New York: BasicBooks.

Gear, G. (1978). Effects of training on teachers' accuracy in identifying gifted children. *Gifted Child Quarterly, 22,* 90–97.

Gilliam, J. E., Carpenter, B. O., & Christensen, J. R. (1996). *Gifted and talented evaluation scales.* Austin, TX: PRO-ED.

Goertzel, V., & Goertzel, M. G. (1962). *Cradles of eminence.* Boston: Little, Brown.

Gruber (1982). *Darwin on man: A psychological study of scientific creativity* (2nd ed.). Chicago: University of Chicago Press.

Guilford, J. P. (1950). Creativity. *American Psychologist, 5,* 444–454.

Jacobs, J. (1971). Effectiveness of teacher and parent identification as a function of school level. *Psychology in the Schools, 9,* 140–142.

Johnsen, S. K. (1997). Assessment beyond definitions. *Peabody Journal of Education, 72,* 136–152.

Johnsen, S. K. (2004a). Evaluating the effectiveness of identification procedures. In S. K. Johnsen (Ed.), *Identifying gifted students: A practical guide* (pp. 133–139). Waco, TX: Prufrock Press.

Johnsen, S. K. (Ed.). (2004b). *Identifying gifted students: A practical guide.* Waco, TX: Prufrock Press.

Johnsen, S. K. (2004c). Making decisions about placement. In S. K. Johnsen (Ed.), *Identifying gifted students: A practical guide* (pp. 107–131). Waco, TX: Prufrock Press.

Johnsen, S. K., & Corn, A. L. (2001). *Screening assessment for gifted elementary students* (2nd ed.). Austin, TX: PRO-ED.

Johnsen, S. K., & Ryser, G. R. (1997). The validity of portfolios in predicting performance in a gifted program. *Journal for the Education of the Gifted, 20,* 253–267.

Johnsen, S. K., Sigler, G., McGregor, G., Snapp, C., & Jackson, M. (1999). *An evaluation of the implementation of language arts programs for gifted students in the Irving ISD.* Irving, TX: Irving Independent School District.

Jolly, J. L., & Hall, J. R. (2004). Technical information regarding assessment. In S. K. Johnsen (Ed.), *Identifying gifted students: A practical guide* (pp. 51–105). Waco, TX: Prufrock Press.

Karnes, F. A. (1991). Leadership and gifted adolescents. In M. Bireley & J. Genshaft (Eds.), *Understanding the gifted adolescent* (pp. 122–138). New York: Teachers College Press.

Karnes, F. A., & Marquardt, R. G. (1991). *Gifted children and the law.* Dayton: Ohio Psychology Press.

Keyser, D., & Sweetland, R. (2004). *Test critiques, Volumes I–XI.* Austin, TX: PRO-ED.

Khatena, J. (1988). *Multitalent assessment records.* Starkville: Mississippi State University.

Khatena, J. (1992). *Gifted: Challenge and response for education.* Itasca, IL: Peacock.

Kulik, J. (2004). Meta-analytic studies of acceleration. In N. Colangelo, S. G. Assouline, & M. U. M. Gross (Eds.), *A nation deceived: How schools hold back America's brightest students* (Vol. II, pp. 13–22). Iowa City, IA: The Connie Belin & Jacqueline N. Blank International Center for Gifted Education and Talent Development.

Landrum, M. S., Callahan, C. M., & Shaklee, B. D. (Eds.). (2001). *Aiming for excellence: Annotations to the NAGC pre-K–grade 12 gifted program standards.* Waco, TX: Prufrock Press.

Maddox, T. (2004). *Tests: A comprehensive reference for assessments in psychology, education, and business* (5th ed.). Austin, TX: PRO-ED.

Murphy, L. L., Plake, B. S., Impara, J. C., & Spies, R. A. (Eds.). (2002). *Tests in print, Volume VI.* Lincoln: University of Nebraska Press.

Perkins, D. N. (1981). *The mind's best work.* Cambridge, MA: Harvard University Press.

Piirto, J. (1999). *Talented children and adults: Their development and education* (2nd ed.). Upper Saddle River, NJ: Merrill.

Renzulli, J. S., Smith, L. H., White, A. J., Callahan, C. M., Hartman, R. K., & Westberg, K. L. (2002). *Scales for rating the behavioral characteristics of superior students.* Mansfield Center, CT: Creative Learning Press.

Rogers, K. B. (2001). *Re-forming gifted education: Matching the program to the child.* Scottsdale, AZ: Great Potential Press.

Ryser, G. R. (2004). Qualitative and quantitative approaches to assessment. In S. K. Johnsen (Ed.), *Identifying gifted students: A practical guide* (pp. 23–40). Waco, TX: Prufrock Press.

Ryser, G. R., & McConnell, K. (2004). *Scales for identifying gifted students.* Waco, TX: Prufrock Press.

Salvia, J., & Ysseldyke, J. E. (2001). *Assessment* (8th ed.). Boston: Houghton-Mifflin

Seashore, C. E., Leavis, D., & Saetveit, J. (1960). *Seashore measures of musical talents.* New York: The Psychological Corporation.

Southern, W. T., & Jones, E. D. (2004). Types of acceleration: Dimensions and Issues. In N. Colangelo, S. G. Assouline, & M. U. M. Gross (Eds.), *A nation deceived: How schools hold back America's brightest students* (Vol. II, pp. 5–12). Iowa City, IA: The Connie Belin & Jacqueline N. Blank International Center for Gifted Education and Talent Development.

Sternberg, R. J. (Ed.). (1988). *The nature of creativity.* Cambridge, England: Cambridge University Press.

Sternberg, R. J., & Davidson, J. E. (Eds.). (1986). *Conceptions of giftedness.* Cambridge, England: Cambridge University Press.

Swassing, R. H. (1985). *Teaching gifted children and adolescents.* Columbus, OH: Merrill.

Tannenbaum, A. J. (1983). *Gifted children: Psychological and educational perspectives.* New York: Macmillan.

Texas Education Agency. (n. d.). *Texas student portfolio.* Austin, TX: Advanced Academic Services.

Tolan, S. S. (1992a). Special problems of highly gifted children. *Understanding Our Gifted, 4*(3), 3, 5.

Tolan, S. S. (1992b). Parents vs. theorists: Dealing with the exceptionally gifted. *Roeper Review, 15,* 14–18.

Torrance, E. P. (1974). *Torrance tests of creative thinking.* Bensenville, IL: Scholastic Testing Service.

Trice, B., & Shannon, B. (2002, April). *Office for Civil Rights: Ensuring equal access to gifted education.* Paper presented at the annual meeting of the Council for Exceptional Children, New York.

U. S. Department of Education, Office of Educational Research and Improvement. (1993). *National excellence: A case for developing America's talent.* Washington, DC: U.S. Government Printing Office.

Wechsler, D. (2003). *Wechsler intelligence scale for children* (4th ed.). San Antonio, TX: The Psychological Corporation.

Whitmore, J. (1980). *Giftedness, conflict, and underachievement.* Boston: Allyn and Bacon.

Appendix
Forms for Use in Implementing the Identification Process

Parent/Guardian Permission for Testing

Student: _____

Grade: _____

School: _____

Date: _____

Your child has been nominated for the gifted and talented program. If your child qualifies for this gifted program, he or she will receive daily services outside the classroom and receive differentiated instruction inside the general education classroom.

Your child will be taking additional assessments to complete the identification process. Please return this form immediately to your school counselor to indicate your permission for additional testing. You will have access to these assessment results, which will become part of your child's permanent record.

If your child is selected for this program, you will be notified and requested to give your permission for participation. Thank you for your interest in your child's educational program.

Sincerely,
Principal

Parent or Guardian _____

Date _____

Parent/Guardian Permission for Placement in Gifted Program

Student: _____

Grade: _____

School: _____

Date: _____

Your child has been recommended for the gifted program. Participation in the gifted program requires written permission of the parent or legal guardian. Please return this form to your school as soon as possible.

I/we approve our child's participation in the gifted program. We understand that an annual assessment will be made of each student's progress. Failure to meet required expectations of the program may result in a committee review to determine continued placement or dismissal.

Parent or Guardian _____

Date _____

Letter to Parents of Child Who Did Not Meet Placement Criteria

Dear Parent(s):

Our school's G/T Screening Committee recently met. Your child was nominated and was carefully considered for placement in the gifted program, but did not meet the district criteria at this time. The committee believes that the general education program may meet his/her needs. Remember that nomination alone suggests that the performance and ability of your child is above average as recognized by teachers and screening instruments.

Your child may be considered for the program at a later date. Please feel free to call the school principal or counselor for any additional information or for a review of your child's test scores. If you feel that there is a basis to appeal the committee's decision, please discuss these concerns with the principal or counselor.

Sincerely,
G/T Program Coordinator

Request for Appeal

Student: _____

Grade: _____

School: _____

Date: _____

Reason for the Appeal:

Parent or guardian's signature _____

Principal's signature _____

Dismissal From the Gifted Program

Student: _____

Grade: _____

School: _____

Date: _____

1. Identify who initiated the dismissal procedure:

2. Briefly summarize the reasons for dismissal.

3. Document conferences that were held to discuss dismissal:
    Dates: Persons Participating:

4. If dismissal is recommended by the G/T teachers, have a committee member sign to indicate dismissal was recommended. The committee must consist of the G/T teacher, principal, parent, and homeroom teacher. Other professionals who know the student should also be involved.

G/T Teacher: _____

Parent(s): _____

Homeroom Teacher: _____

Other: _____

Principal's Signature: _____ Date:_____

Furlough Request From Gifted Program

_____, a gifted
student in grade _____, has requested a furlough from the
gifted program at _____.

Here are the circumstances that suggest a furlough is appropriate at this time:

The student plans to return to the gifted program on _____.

G/T Teacher: _____

Parent(s): _____

Student: _____

Principal: _____

Other: _____

Date: _____

About the Author

Susan K. Johnsen is a professor in the Department of Educational Psychology at Baylor University. She directs and teaches courses in gifted education at the undergraduate and graduate levels. She is editor of *Gifted Child Today* and serves on the editorial boards of *Gifted Child Quarterly* and *The Journal of Secondary Gifted Education*. She is the coauthor of the *Independent Study Program* and three tests that are used in identifying gifted students: Test of Mathematical Abilities for Gifted Students (TOMAGS), Test of Nonverbal Intelligence (TONI-3), and the Screening Assessment for Gifted Students (SAGES-2). She has published numerous articles and is a frequent presenter at state, national, and international conferences. She is past-president of the Texas Association for the Gifted and Talented and serves on the board of the The Association for Gifted, a division of the Council for Exceptional Children.

Printed in the United States
by Baker & Taylor Publisher Services